UNVEILING THE SECRETS OF SUCCESSFUL BLOGGING

INSIDER TIPS AND TRICKS

CYRIL LAKES

Contents

CHAPTER ONE 3

INTRODUCTION 3

    The Growth of Blogging 5

    The Value of Effective Blogging 10

    Comprehending Blogging 16

CHAPTER TWO 25

    Identifying Your Specialization 25

    Organizing Your Blog 31

    Creating Engaging Content 37

    Developing and Expanding Your Audience 43

    Strategies for Monetization 49

CHAPTER THREE 52

    Resources & Tools for Blogging 55

    Taking Care of Your Blog 63

    Overcoming Obstacles 70

CHAPTER FOUR 76

    A Legal and Ethical Perspective 78

    Future Blogging Trends 83

    Summary 89

THE END 93

CHAPTER ONE

INTRODUCTION

Blogging is one of the most effective digital platforms for communication, creativity, and self-expression on the internet. Blogs have changed from being personal diaries to becoming professional platforms, becoming vibrant places where people and companies can share their knowledge, experiences, and insights with the world.

However, what distinguishes a prosperous blog from the plethora of voices demanding recognition on the internet? What are the keys to creating a successful blog that attracts readers, grows a devoted following, and makes a significant impact?

We will go out on a quest to discover the keys to profitable blogging with this guide, delving into the methods, approaches, and ideas that enable bloggers to fulfill their ambitions and reach their objectives. This guide is your road map to realizing the full potential of blogging success, whether you're an experienced writer hoping to expand your reach or a novice keen to establish yourself online.

Come explore the art and science of blogging with us as we explore the tactics that, in the constantly changing world of online content creation, generate community, impact, and drive engagement. This tutorial will provide you the skills and knowledge you need to succeed in the fast-paced world of blogging, from creating engaging material to grasping promotion and monetization techniques.

Prepare to dive into your creativity, stoke your enthusiasm, and take a voyage of discovery as we reveal the trade secrets of profitable blogging. Your voice has the ability to inspire, educate, and change the world the digital stage is waiting for you. Together, let's explore the game-changing possibilities of exceptional blogging.

The Growth of Blogging

When websites were static and there was no opportunity for online interaction in the early days of the internet, blogging became a groundbreaking medium for individual expression and community involvement. Online journals and diaries soon gave way to a vibrant platform for knowledge sharing, idea exchange, and story telling with a worldwide audience.

There are various reasons why blogging has become more popular:

Accessibility: Anyone with an internet connection can now generate and publish content without the need for technical expertise or coding knowledge thanks to the introduction of user-friendly blogging platforms like Blogger and WordPress. Through the democratization of publishing, people from all walks of life were able to express themselves and their viewpoints to a global audience.

Interactivity: Blogs enabled two-way communication and engagement between authors and readers, in contrast to traditional media formats like newspapers or magazines. Readers were able to interact directly with content providers through email subscriptions, social sharing buttons, and comment areas, which promoted a sense of community and cooperation.

Niche Communities: Through blogging, people were able to carve out areas on the huge internet that catered to certain interests, hobbies, or industries. Bloggers who focused on food, fashion, technology, or travel discovered that their niche audiences were enthusiastic about the subjects they covered, which led to lively communities and devoted fan bases.

Authenticity and Personalization: In contrast to corporate media platforms, blogs provided a more personal and intimate voice, enabling writers to express their thoughts, experiences, and personal tales in their own words. Readers looking for real connections and accessible information in an increasingly digital world found this authenticity appealing.

Possibilities for Monetization: As blogging gained popularity, it also offered profitable chances for revenue generation via product sales, affiliate marketing, sponsorships, and advertising. Profiting from their enthusiasm, successful bloggers might monetize their platforms while preserving their authenticity and trustworthiness.

Influence and Authority: Prosperous bloggers gained the respect, credibility, and authority of their audiences by positioning themselves as thought leaders and influencers in their respective fields over time. Their evaluations, suggestions, and observations were influential and influenced market and consumer trends.

Blogging is still a thriving, dynamic medium today, adjusting to shifting consumer tastes, technological advancements, and industry trends. In the digital age, blogging is a strong tool for content marketing, brand promotion, and audience engagement for both individuals and businesses, regardless of blogging experience level.

One thing is evident as we see blogging continue to develop: it has a profoundly positive influence on culture, community, and communication. The popularity of blogging has changed how people produce, consume, and engage with material online by enabling them to tell their stories, give their voices more weight, and connect with like-minded people around the world.

The Value of Effective Blogging

Successful blogging has many advantages and opportunities for people, businesses, and communities that go far beyond just having a digital presence. Here's a thorough examination of the reasons why blogging success matters:

A Medium for Self-Expression: Blogging gives people a way to freely express their ideas, opinions, thoughts, and creativity. It acts as a digital journal that encourages self-expression and authenticity by allowing users to share their thoughts, feelings, and personal tales with a worldwide audience.

Developing Authority and Influence: People can become thought leaders, influencers, and experts in their fields through blogging successfully. Bloggers can develop authority, credibility, and influence in their profession by providing insightful information, interacting with their audience, and creating high-quality content on a regular basis.

Building Communities: Blogs can be used as focal points to bring like-minded people together online who have similar hobbies, interests, or aspirations. Bloggers have the ability to cultivate a sense of community and camaraderie among their readers by means of comments, discussions, and social media sharing.

Blogging is an effective strategy for businesses and professionals to use for content marketing and brand building. Businesses may draw in, hold on to, and attract customers while promoting their brand identity and values by producing educational, interesting, and pertinent content that speaks to the needs and interests of their target audience.

Increasing Search Engine Optimization (SEO) Rankings and Organic Website Traffic: Blogging is essential for boosting search engine optimization (SEO) rankings and organic website traffic. Published on a blog, new, pertinent, and keyword-rich content can draw readers in, improve online discoverability, and raise website visibility all of which can lead to more leads, conversions, and sales.

Possibilities for Income Generation: Profitable blogs include a range of revenue streams for both individuals and companies, such as sponsorships, advertising, affiliate marketing, product sales, and subscriptions to premium content. By using their readership, influence, and experience, bloggers can monetize their online platforms and generate passive revenue streams.

Professional Development: By refining writing, communication, research, and marketing skills, blogging can help with both personal and professional development. The skills and information that bloggers get from navigating the complexities of content creation, audience engagement, and digital marketing are invaluable and can be applied to various aspects of their personal and professional lives.

Educational Resource: Blogs are excellent sources of knowledge where readers may obtain guides, instructions, explanations, and information on a variety of subjects. For readers looking for information and direction, blogs offer a wealth of knowledge and inspiration on everything from DIY projects and lifestyle advice to industry trends and best practices.

Social influence and Advocacy: By spreading awareness, supporting causes, and uniting communities around significant issues, well-run blogs have the power to have a positive social influence and promote good change. Bloggers have the ability to use their platforms to dispel prejudices, give voice to underrepresented groups, and advance equality and social justice.

Personal Satisfaction and Fulfillment: Above all, blogging success provides a feeling of accomplishment, satisfaction, and personal fulfillment. Blogging enables people to follow their interests, express themselves honestly, and have a real impact on the world whether it's by sharing a passion, changing the world, or reaching career milestones.

A successful blog involves more than just producing material; it also involves networking, knowledge sharing, having an influence, and achieving both personal and professional objectives. Through the effective use of blogging, people and companies may increase their visibility online, reach a wider audience, and make a lasting impression.

Comprehending Blogging

Knowing blogging is knowing its nature, function, and dynamics in the online environment. Let's examine the essential elements of comprehending blogging:

The process of generating and posting content on a blog, which is a frequently updated website or online platform where people or organizations share knowledge, insights, anecdotes, or expertise, is known as blogging. Posts on blogs are usually arranged in reverse chronological order, with the most recent entries showing up first.

Goals and objectives of the blogger or organization determine the purpose of blogging, which varies. Typical goals consist of:

Personal Expression: Blogging is a popular way for people to share their thoughts, experiences, and personal tales with a larger audience.

Information Sharing: In order to meet readers' information demands, blogs provide forums for the exchange of knowledge, information, and experience on a variety of subjects or interests.

Building Communities: Blogs help to create online communities where people who share similar interests may meet, communicate, and have conversations about their common interests or passions.

information Marketing: By offering useful and pertinent information that speaks to their needs and interests, bloggers help businesses and professionals draw in, hold on to, and grow their client base.

Brand Building: By exhibiting the principles, skills, and products and services of people, companies, or organizations, blogs are essential for increasing brand awareness, credibility, and authority.

Components of a Blog: There are various essential components that make up a normal blog, such as:

Posts: Singular pieces of writing that are posted on the blog and cover a variety of subjects or themes.

Comments: Areas where readers can debate the content, pose questions, or offer comments.

Posts can be categorized and classified using categories and tags, which are organizational tools that are based on subjects, themes, or keywords.

Archives: A list of previous articles arranged in a chronological order that lets users peruse older items.

Sidebar Widgets: Extra elements tacked on to the side of the blog layout, including search bars, social media buttons, or subscription forms.

Types of Blogs: Blogs are available in a variety of formats and styles to suit a range of audiences, interests, and goals. Typical blog formats consist of:

Personal blogs: Diaries or notebooks in which people write about their own experiences, insights, and tales.

Blogs with a narrow concentration, such as those about technology, travel, gastronomy, fashion, or health, are known as niche blogs.

Business blogs: Companies and organizations utilize corporate or professional blogs for branding, marketing, and consumer interaction.

Blogs that provide news, comments on current affairs, and analysis of social, political, and cultural topics are known as news blogs.

Blogs that review books, movies, services, goods, or other interesting stuff are known as review blogs.

Blogging Platforms: You can create and host blogs on a number of different blogging platforms, such as:

WordPress: renowned for its adaptability, rich plugin ecosystem, and customization options, this blogging platform is the most popular and commonly used one.

Blogger: A straightforward blogging platform owned by Google that provides easy-to-use tools for content creation and publication.

Medium: A publishing platform with social sharing tools and an audience that is already there, with an emphasis on excellent writing and narrative.

Tumblr: A microblogging site that lets users publish multimedia content in an eye-catching way by fusing social networking with traditional blogging.

Best Practices: Following best practices that optimize reach, engagement, and effect is crucial for blogging success. Among the finest practices are:

Consistency: To keep readers interested and coming back for more, consistently post high-quality content.

Authenticity: In your writing, voice, and relationships with readers, be sincere, open, and real.

Engagement: Promote audience participation by answering questions, starting conversations, and asking for comments.

SEO Optimization: Use meta tags, descriptive titles and headings, and pertinent keywords to make your blog entries more search engine friendly.

Promotion: To increase your readership and reach a wider audience, use email newsletters, social networking, guest posting, and partnerships with other bloggers to promote your blog material.

Monetization: To make money from your site, investigate monetization techniques like product sales, affiliate marketing, sponsorships, and advertising.

CHAPTER TWO

Understanding blogging entails being aware of its goals, elements, formats, platforms, and most effective methods. Learning the foundations of blogging is crucial for producing engaging material, growing an audience, and accomplishing your blogging objectives, regardless of experience level.

Identifying Your Specialization

Discovering your area of expertise is essential to learning the trade secrets of profitable blogging. Your blog's niche helps you stand out in a crowded online space by defining its purpose, readership, and distinctive value offer. Here's how to identify your blogging niche so you can make money:

Determine Your Interests and Passions: To begin, decide which themes, topics, or hobbies you are truly interested in and enthusiastic about. To find possible niche ideas that fit with your beliefs and interests, consider your experiences, talents, interests, and hobbies.

Analyze Market Demand: Use resources like Google Trends, keyword research tools, and social media analytics to investigate audience interest and market demand for possible niche themes. To make sure there is a market for your material, seek out specialized prospects with a substantial audience and increasing interest.

Examine Competition: By looking at current blogs, websites, and content producers in those fields, you may determine the degree of competition and saturation in potential niche markets. Seek for openings, underutilized audience niches, or ways to set your blog apart from rivals.

Reduce Your attention: To create a distinct place inside your selected niche, reduce your attention to a single topic, theme, or audience group. Since niche blogging depends on specialization and specificity, avoid being overly general or generic.

Think About Your Expertise and Unique Perspective: To set your blog apart from the competition and give your readers insightful content, make the most of your knowledge, experience, expertise, and unique perspective. Offer your knowledge, anecdotes from your life, and observations that distinguish your blog and speak to your intended readership.

Determine Your Target Audience: Using information on demographics, interests, requirements, and preferences, create an ideal reader persona or target audience. Recognize their problems, obstacles, and driving forces in order to customize your messaging and content to appeal to them and meet their particular needs.

Test and Validate Your Niche: To determine audience interest and feedback, test your niche concept by producing sample material, doing polls, or starting a trial blog. Keep an eye on social shares, comments, and engagement metrics to gauge the potential and viability of your niche.

Refine and Adapt: Be open to changing your specialty over time in response to audience feedback, industry developments, and your own changing passions and areas of expertise. To maintain long-term relevance and success, remain flexible and adaptable to changes in the blogging scene.

Maintaining inspiration and innovation requires passion, but you should also take into account the possible profitability and monetization opportunities in your chosen specialty. Find a balance between following subjects you are enthusiastic about and spotting profitable niche markets.

Remain True to Your True Voice: In the end, maintaining your true voice, values, and personality is what makes niche blogging effective. Establish credibility and trust with your audience by being sincere, open, and consistent in the material you create.

These techniques will help you find a niche that fits your hobbies, connects with your audience, and positions you for success in the blogging industry. Remember to exercise caution while choosing a topic. Always keep in mind that identifying your niche is a continuous process of investigation, testing, and improvement; thus, welcome the adventure and remain dedicated to providing value to your audience.

Organizing Your Blog

In order to ensure that your content strategy is in line with your goals, audience, and specialty, planning your blog is an essential first step towards building a successful blog. This is a thorough approach to efficiently organizing your blog:

Establish Your Objectives: To begin, make sure your blog's overall aims and objectives are clear. Do you want to become recognized as an expert in your field, create leads for your company, monetize your platform, or just spread your love around? Your whole blogging approach, including content strategy, will be guided by your clearly defined goals.

Determine Your Target Audience: Make sure you know who your target audience is by developing thorough reader personas that take into account their demographics, hobbies, preferences, and areas of suffering. This will enable you to more successfully cater your content to your audience's unique requirements and interests and make it resonate with them.

Select Your Niche: Focus on your area of interest, area of competence, audience analysis, and market need. Within your larger niche, pick a focused subject, theme, or approach that will help you stand out from the competition and establish a stronger connection with your target market.

Create Your Content Strategy: List potential topics, content types, and publication schedules to help you organize your content strategy. Think about the kinds of content—how-to manuals, listicles, case studies, interviews, product reviews, or personal narratives—that your audience will find engaging. To plan your content schedule and guarantee consistency in publication, make an editorial calendar.

Keyword Research: Find pertinent subjects and search phrases that members of your target audience are using to your advantage by conducting keyword research. To help you with your content production and SEO, use tools such as Google Keyword Planner, SEMrush, or Ahrefs to find high-volume keywords, long-tail keywords, and related themes.

Establish a Consistent Brand Identity: Craft a blog identity that encompasses your site's name, logo, color palette, typography, and visual components. Your brand identity should appeal to your target market, provide a distinctive and recognizable brand presence, and represent your niche, personality, and values.

Establish Your Blogging Platform: Select a blogging platform based on your requirements, tastes, and level of technical proficiency. Popular choices include of Medium, Wix, WordPress, and Blogger. Make your audience's experience on your blog both visually appealing and easy to use by customizing the layout and style.

Make a material Calendar: Arrange your material by prearranging the themes, release dates, and marketing campaigns. When creating your content calendar, take into account industry events, holidays, and seasonal patterns to ensure that it is timely and relevant.

Determine Your Voice and Tone: To guarantee consistency in your writing style and messaging throughout all of your blog entries, identify your brand's voice and tone. Your writing should convey your brand's identity and connect with your audience whether you want to write in an informal, conversational style or a more formal, authoritative one.

Distribution and Promotion: Create a plan for distribution and promotion to increase the visibility of your blog posts and draw in readers. To improve reader engagement and boost traffic to your site, use influencer partnerships, email newsletters, social media platforms, guest blogging, and SEO strategies.

Monitor and Measure Performance: Track important metrics like website traffic, engagement, and conversions by utilizing analytics tools like Google Analytics or social media analytics. Keep an eye on how well your blog pieces are performing, examine reader comments, and tweak your content strategy in light of new information and data-driven choices.

By following these guidelines and devoting time to thoughtful blog preparation, you'll position yourself for success and lay the groundwork for developing a successful, long-lasting blog that connects with readers, accomplishes your objectives, and leaves a lasting impression in your niche.

Creating Engaging Content

Creating engaging material is crucial to learning the trade secrets of profitable blogging. Not only can excellent content draw in and hold the attention of readers, but it also establishes your authority, fosters trust, and increases blog traffic.

The following advice can help you produce engaging content:

Know Your Audience: Recognize the interests, inclinations, and problems of your target market. Make sure your material speaks to their wants, solves their problems, and resonates with them by offering insightful information.

Offer Specialized Viewpoints, Insights, or Experiences to Differentiate Your Content from the Competition. Strive to provide unique, fresh content that improves the lives of your readers rather than simply restating information that is already publicly accessible.

Put Quality before Quantity: When producing content, put quality before quantity. Rather than publishing a constant stream of content, concentrate on crafting insightful, well-written, and thoroughly researched pieces that showcase your proficiency and authority within your industry.

Tell Captivating Stories: To make your material more relatable and engaging, employ storytelling tactics. Use case studies, personal tales, or real-world examples to support your arguments and emotionally engage your audience.

Employ Attention-Grabbing Headlines: Write headlines that will draw readers in and encourage them to click through to your information. To get readers to read your blog article further, use attention-grabbing headlines, statistics, queries, or intriguing assertions.

Write Captivating openers: Grab readers' attention right away and establish the tone for the remainder of your material with captivating openers. To grab readers' attention, ask a thought-provoking question, provide an eye-opening statistic, or offer a gripping narrative.

Offer Practical, Actionable Takeaways: Provide readers with guidance, techniques, or tips that they can instantly put into practice in their own life. Offer readers checklists, templates, or step-by-step instructions so they can put your thoughts into practice and see real results.

Employ Visuals and Multimedia: To improve your content and break up lengthy text passages, use visuals like photos, infographics, videos, or slideshows. Images not only improve the visual attractiveness of your material but also aid in the more efficient delivery of information.

Optimize for Readability: To make your information easier to skim and understand, format it with bullet points, subheadings, short paragraphs, and white space. Don't use jargon or technical phrases that could confuse readers; instead, speak clearly and succinctly.

Encourage Interaction: At the conclusion of your blog entries, provide an invitation to readers to leave comments, queries, and other feedback. In order to build a feeling of community and involvement around your content, quickly reply to reader comments and encourage dialogue.

Update and Refresh Content: To maintain your current content current, correct, and relevant, it should be updated and refreshed on a regular basis. To keep your material relevant and visible over time, update out-of-date information, add fresh perspectives or examples, and optimize for search engines.

Be Consistent: To keep your audience interested and returning for more, stick to a regular posting schedule. Whether you post once a week, twice a week, or once a month, consistency is essential for gaining momentum, drawing visitors, and eventually expanding your blog.

By putting these suggestions into practice and concentrating on producing interesting, worthwhile content, you'll improve the caliber and effect of your blog, draw in a devoted readership, and discover the keys to blogging success.

Developing and Expanding Your Audience

Discovering the keys to blogging success requires developing and expanding your following. In addition to expanding your blog's visibility and reach, a devoted and active readership generates traffic, offers insightful criticism, and creates opportunities for advertising. Here are some tips for developing and expanding your audience:

Know Your Audience: Recognize the characteristics, hobbies, tastes, and problems of your target market. Utilize social media insights, surveys, analytics tools, and audience research to learn more about the requirements and behaviors of your target audience.

Provide Useful material: Put your energy into producing useful material that appeals to your target audience. Offer answers to their queries, problem-solving solutions, and insightful commentary, pointers, or counsel that takes into account their requirements and interests.

Describe Your Special Value Proposition: Set yourself apart from the competition by emphasizing your special value proposition. Determine what makes your blog unique from others in your niche and convey that information to your readers in an impactful way.

Optimize for SEO: By making your content more search engine friendly, you may increase the visibility and discoverability of your blog. Find appropriate keywords through keyword research, then carefully include them to the titles, meta descriptions, headings, and body of your blog posts.

Promote Your Content: To reach a larger audience, actively promote the content of your blog on a variety of platforms. To spread the word about your content and draw people to your site, make use of influencer partnerships, email newsletters, guest blogging, social media platforms, and online forums.

Engage Your Audience: Encourage audience participation by answering queries, comments, and criticism on your blog and social media pages. To foster a feeling of community and involvement, ask for feedback, have debates, and involve your audience in the content development process.

Create an Email List: Create a list of subscribers to your blog's email address who would like to receive updates and information. Provide enticements to readers to join your email list and follow your blog, such as lead magnets, access to unique content, or discounts.

Use Social Media: Make use of social media channels to increase the visibility of your blog and interact with readers. To expand your reach and draw in new readers, share your blog entries, engage with followers, join pertinent groups and communities, and take part in debates.

Network and Collaborate: To increase your audience and reach, network with other bloggers, influencers, and business experts in your niche. Work together on podcasts, guest blogs, interviews, or collaborative projects to reach each other's audiences and expand your fan base.

Analyze Data and Modify Plans: Make use of analytics tools to keep tabs on important data including audience demographics, website traffic, engagement, and conversion rates. Keep an eye on how well your content and marketing are performing, and modify your plans in light of new information and data-driven choices.

Offer Value-Added Services: Give your audience access to extra resources or value-added services like webinars, courses, ebooks, or private membership groups. To encourage participation and support, provide devoted subscribers or customers with exclusive content or benefits.

Be Patient and Persistent: It takes time, patience, and persistence to establish and grow an audience. Even when things are difficult or growth is slow, never waver from your commitment to publishing high-quality content, interacting with readers, and advertising your blog.

You can discover the keys to blogging success and progressively increase the number of people who visit your site by putting these tactics into practice and concentrating on developing deep relationships with your readers. Keep in mind to be genuine, receptive, and flexible as you grow and develop your readership and following.

Strategies for Monetization

Discovering the techniques of profitable blogging requires you to monetize your site in order to transform your hobby into a source of revenue. The following are some successful blog monetization techniques:

Advertising: Use ad networks like Google AdSense, Media.net, or AdThrive to place adverts on your site in order to make money. To optimize visibility and clicks, place native, text, or banner advertising strategically across your content or sidebar.

Brand Partnerships and Sponsorships: Work with businesses, brands, or sponsors to produce sponsored posts, product reviews, or sponsored material for your site. Reach out to sponsors, affiliates, or brand ambassadors to promote goods and services that fit your audience and niche.

Promote affiliate goods and services on your blog to earn commissions for each sale or referral made using your affiliate links. This is known as affiliate marketing. Join affiliate networks that are pertinent to your industry, write product and service reviews, provide referrals, and incorporate affiliate links into your writing.

Selling Digital Goods: Produce and market digital goods that are relevant to your specialty, such as ebooks, online courses, workshops, manuals, templates, or printables. Convert your experience, knowledge, or abilities into useful digital products that address the issues or offer new perspectives to your target market.

Membership and Subscription Services: Using subscription services like Patreon, Substack, or Memberful, provide subscribers or patrons with premium material, special access, or membership benefits. To encourage memberships, offer exclusive content, live Q&A sessions, exclusive communities, or extra stuff.

Freelancing and Consulting Services: Make use of your experience, education, or abilities to provide clients in your specialty with coaching, consulting, or freelancing services. Depending on your area of expertise, provide specialized services, one-on-one coaching sessions, or consultation packages.

CHAPTER THREE

Selling Physical Goods: Take up the business of selling tangible goods like branded goods, niche-related goods, or general stuff. Produce and market branded goods, clothing, accessories, and other items that are in line with your brand identity and appeal to your target market.

Obtain speaking engagements, collaborations, and sponsorships for conferences, webinars, workshops, and other events that are relevant to your area of expertise. To demonstrate your knowledge and draw sponsors, offer to lead panel discussions, conduct workshops, or speak at industry events.

Paywalls and Premium Content: If you want to grant readers access to your blog's gated or premium content, you should put in place a paywall or subscription model. Provide comprehensive manuals, analysis, case studies, or exclusive interviews that are only accessible through a paywall in order to encourage memberships and create recurring income.

Donations & Crowdfunding: Use websites like Patreon, Buy Me a Coffee, or PayPal to collect donations from your audience or to launch crowdfunding campaigns. In order to express their gratitude for your material, readers should be encouraged to support your site financially by making donations or by participating in your crowdsourcing effort.

Selling Ad Space Directly: If you want to reach your audience, you can sell ad space directly to sponsors or advertisers. For a set charge or monthly retainer, negotiate banner ad slots on your site, sponsored content opportunities, or customized advertising packages.

E-commerce Integration: To sell goods to your readers directly, incorporate e-commerce features into your blog. Create a shopping cart, checkout process, or online store to sell goods, services, or digital or tangible objects straight from your blog.

You may enhance your blog's earning potential and discover the keys to successful blogging by widening your monetization techniques and utilizing a variety of money streams. Try out several revenue streams, monitor your progress, and modify your tactics according to what resonates most with your target market.

Resources & Tools for Blogging

Using the appropriate tools and resources can greatly improve your blogging experience overall, as well as your efficiency and productivity, to help you unlock the secrets of successful blogging. A selection of vital tools and resources for bloggers is provided below:

Systems for managing content (CMS):

The most well-liked and adaptable content management system (CMS) for bloggers is WordPress, which has an intuitive user interface, themes, and plugins.

Blogger: Google's user-friendly blogging platform with simple connection with Google services and basic blogging functionality.

Platforms for Hosting Websites:

WordPress recommends Bluehost, a dependable hosting company with cost-effective hosting packages and round-the-clock customer service.

SiteGround: Well-known for its quick loading times, security features, and top-notch customer support, this hosting provider is perfect for bloggers looking for high-performance capabilities.

Tools for Editing and Creating Content:

Grammarly: A writing tool that ensures your blog entries are polished and error-free by checking for spelling, grammar, and punctuation mistakes.

Hemingway Editor: It makes information clearer and more succinct by emphasizing the use of adverbs, passive voice, and complicated phrases.

Canva: A graphic design tool that lets you use drag-and-drop capabilities and configurable templates to create aesthetically appealing graphics, social media postings, and blog post images.

Tools for Researching Keywords:

With the aid of Google Keyword Planner, you can find pertinent keywords and data on search volume to enhance SEO and guide your content strategy.

SEMrush: Provides thorough keyword research, competitive analysis, and SEO insights to help you improve the content of your blog and drive more natural traffic.

Tools for tracking and analytics:

Google Analytics: Gives you comprehensive information about the traffic to your website, the demographics of your readership, and user behavior. This information helps you assess the effectiveness of your blog and pinpoint areas for development.

WordPress' Jetpack plugin provides performance optimization tools, security features, and site analytics so you can monitor and improve your blog's performance right within WordPress.

Platforms for Email Marketing:

Easily create and send newsletters, automate email campaigns, and cultivate subscriber lists to interact with your audience using Mailchimp, an intuitive email marketing platform.

ConvertKit: Developed especially for bloggers and content producers, this platform offers segmentation, sophisticated email automation, and configurable opt-in forms to help you build relationships with your subscribers and expand your email list.

Tools for Social Media Management:

Hootsuite: Helps you increase your social media presence by letting you plan, publish, and manage posts on several platforms, as well as track engagement and keep an eye on conversations.

Buffer: Makes social media posting, analytics, and interaction easier. It lets you schedule and plan posts, monitor performance, and assess outcomes to make the most out of your social media strategy.

Plugins for search engine optimization (SEO):

Yoast SEO: An effective WordPress plugin that raises your blog's exposure and search engine ranks by offering on-page SEO analysis, optimization suggestions, and XML sitemap creation.

All in One SEO Pack: This tool helps you improve your blog for search engines and has features comparable to Yoast SEO, such as social media integration, XML sitemap support, and meta tag optimization.

Online forums and communities:

Reddit: A well-liked forum where you can interact with specialized groups, take part in conversations, and post links to your blog posts to draw in targeted readers and develop connections with others who share your interests.

Quora: A question-and-answer site where you can answer inquiries about your specialty, offer insightful commentary, and position your blog as a reliable source of knowledge.

Courses and Resources for Education:

You can improve your blogging abilities and expertise by taking use of Udemy's extensive selection of blogging courses, which cover subjects like content production, SEO, email marketing, monetization tactics, and more.

With the support of industry professionals, Skillshare offers access to blogging workshops, tutorials, and classes that can help you learn new methods, tools, and approaches for expanding your blog and readership.

You may gain more success and impact in the digital sphere by improving your blogging game, streamlining your workflow, and making the most of your content strategy by skillfully utilizing these blogging tools and services.

Taking Care of Your Blog

Effective blog management is crucial to the long-term success, stability, and expansion of your site. The following are some essential elements of effective blog management:

Planning and Producing Content:

Plan your content schedule, including themes, release dates, and promotion tactics, by creating an editorial calendar.

To make sure your content strategy is sound and that your pieces are engaging to your target audience, do some research on trends and keywords.

Tasks related to content development can be completed in batches to improve workflow and uniformity in publishing.

Updating and maintaining websites:

Update the themes, plugins, and software on your site on a regular basis to guarantee compatibility, security, and optimum performance.

Make regular backups of your website to protect it against technical problems or data loss.

Keep an eye on the usability and speed of your website and adjust as needed to improve both SEO and user experience.

Participation in Establishing a Community:

In order to encourage participation and establish a rapport with your audience, reply to emails, comments, and social media messages as soon as possible.

Promote user-generated content to engage your audience in the process of creating new material, such as guest pieces or reader submissions.

To increase your network and reach, take part in social media groups, forums, and online communities that are relevant to your niche.

Optimization of Search Engines (SEO):

To raise your blog posts' organic traffic and search engine rankings, make sure they have the right headings, meta descriptions, and keywords.

Using tools such as Google Analytics, track SEO performance and modify your strategy according on important metrics and insights.

Increase the authority and exposure of your blog in search engine results by creating high-quality backlinks from reliable websites.

Revenue Generation and Monetization:

Investigate several monetization techniques, including sponsored content, affiliate marketing, advertising, and digital product sales, to diversify your sources of income.

To optimize revenue potential, always assess the effectiveness of your monetization activities and test out new tactics.

To maintain credibility and trust with your audience, be honest and transparent in your monetization strategies.

Analytics and Monitoring of Performance:

Track important variables like website traffic, engagement, conversion rates, and audience demographics with analytics tools.

Examine performance data to find patterns, trends, and areas where your monetization, promotion, and content initiatives need to be improved.

Establish clear objectives and benchmarks for the development and growth of your blog, then evaluate your progress toward these goals on a regular basis.

Legal and Conformity Aspects to Take Into Account:

To protect both yourself and your audience, be sure that all applicable rules and regulations such as those pertaining to copyright, privacy, and data protection are followed.

Provide readers with information about your rules and practices by including relevant legal pages on your blog, such as a disclaimer, terms of service, and privacy policy.

Keep yourself updated on regulatory changes and industry advancements that could affect your blog, and modify your procedures as necessary.

Productivity and Time Management:

Set priorities for your work and set out certain time for administrative, content production, promotion, and blog management.

Reduce distractions and successfully manage your calendar by utilizing productivity tools and practices like time blocking.

To reduce your workload, assign projects or contract out specific duties, including administrative or graphic design labor, to independent contractors or virtual assistants.

Your blog's long-term success, longevity, and influence in the always changing digital scene can be guaranteed by putting these tactics into practice and keeping a proactive attitude to blog management. Review your objectives, plans, and procedures frequently in order to adjust to new opportunities and trends. You should also keep coming up with new ideas and expanding your blog over time.

Overcoming Obstacles

Uncovering the secrets of successful blogging requires overcoming obstacles. While navigating the ever-changing blogging environment, you will probably run into a number of roadblocks that could prevent you from moving forward. The following are some typical problems that bloggers go into, along with solutions:

Writer's Block: This can hinder your blogging momentum if you are having trouble coming up with fresh ideas or content. Defy writer's block with:

taking pauses to rejuvenate and reinvigorate your ideas.

participating in idea generation activities or brainstorming sessions.

looking into novel subjects, viewpoints, or forms in order to get inspired.

working along with other content producers or bloggers to get new ideas.

Lack of Engagement and Traffic: It can be difficult to grow a blog's following and draw readers, particularly in a cutthroat online world. Defeat this obstacle by:

putting money into search engine optimization (SEO) to raise the exposure and search engine rankings of your blog.

To reach a larger audience, promote your material on forums, online communities, and social media sites.

interacting with your audience on social media, in emails, and in comments to create connections and relationships.

partnering with industry experts, influencers, or guest bloggers to reach a wider audience and gain access to their followers.

Challenges with Monetization: Earning money from your blog might be difficult, particularly in the beginning. Overcome difficulties with monetization by:

experimenting with several monetization techniques and revenue stream diversification, including affiliate marketing, digital product sales, sponsored content, and advertising.

utilizing community building activities, high-quality content, and engagement strategies to cultivate a devoted and active audience in order to draw sponsors, advertising, and paying clients.

To optimize revenue potential, keep assessing and refining your monetization strategies in light of audience input, industry trends, and performance data.

Time Management and Burnout: Attempting to balance blogging with other commitments and responsibilities might cause problems with time management and burnout. Overcome difficulties with time management by:

Setting realistic timelines and priorities for your blog-related activities.

Setting up a blogging regimen or timetable and following it religiously will help you stay consistent and productive.

To reduce your workload, assign duties or outsource specific obligations to virtual assistants or freelancers, such as content development, design, or administrative labor.

You may avoid burnout and preserve your physical and emotional health by setting limits, taking regular breaks, and engaging in self-care.

Technical Difficulties and Website Issues: Your blogging endeavors may be impeded by resolving technical problems, website outages, or maintenance concerns. Overcome difficulties with technology by:

proactively maintaining, updating, and implementing security measures for websites to avert possible problems.

learning some fundamental troubleshooting methods, or when issues arise, contacting technical support or internet resources for assistance.

CHAPTER FOUR

Making regular backups of your website will reduce the possibility of data loss or interruptions in the event of technical malfunctions or security breaches.

Comparison and Imposter Syndrome: Your drive and self-esteem may suffer if you compare yourself to other bloggers or feel unworthy. Get past the imposter syndrome and comparison by:

putting more emphasis on your own development, progress, and advancement than on how you compare to other people.

Celebrating your victories, no matter how minor, will help you feel more confident and good about yourself.

surrounding oneself with a network of peers, mentors, and other bloggers who are willing to assist you and provide insight, counsel, and encouragement.

Keeping in mind that everyone begins somewhere and that blogging requires persistence, patience, and time.

You can better manage the ups and downs of blogging and learn the keys to success in the blogging industry by recognizing these obstacles and putting tactics in place to overcome them. Remain resilient, flexible, and dedicated to your objectives. Additionally, don't be hesitant to ask for help or advice when you need it.

A Legal and Ethical Perspective

Following the law and moral principles is essential while sharing the secrets of profitable blogging in order to safeguard your audience, your reputation, and yourself. The following are some important moral and legal guidelines for bloggers:

Copyright and Intellectual Property: Comply with copyright rules by giving due credit to content that has been sourced from other creators and, if required, seeking permission. A copyrighted image, text, or video should not be used without authorization or the appropriate licensing.

Plagiarism and Attribution: Provide unique content while avoiding plagiarism by giving due credit to your sources. When citing or quoting another blogger's, author's, or creator's work in your blog entries, give them credit.

Privacy and Data Protection: Adhere to data protection laws, such as the California Consumer Privacy Act (CCPA) and the General Data Protection Regulation (GDPR), by putting in place privacy policies, cookie notifications, and consent processes that safeguard the privacy of your audience. Before gathering, keeping, or using your visitors' or subscribers' personal information, get their express consent.

Disclosure and Transparency: Whenever you include sponsored partnerships, sponsorships, affiliate relationships, or endorsements in your material, be sure to disclose them to your audience. Any financial interests, conflicts of interest, or significant relationships that might affect your advice or opinions should be declared up front.

Accuracy and Fact-Checking: Prior to publishing, double-check sources for information and confirm assertions to make sure your blog articles are accurate and reliable. Provide evidence for your statements and claims in the form of citations, references, or links to reliable sources.

Defamation and Libel: Refrain from posting inaccurate or defamatory remarks about people, companies, or groups on your site. Avoid posting anything that can damage someone's reputation, violate their privacy, or have legal ramifications.

Terms of Service, Terms of Use, and Disclaimers: Using terms of service, terms of use, or disclaimers, clearly state the terms of use, disclaimers, and limitations of liability governing your blog. Outline the goals, restrictions, and obligations related to accessing or making use of the services and content on your blog.

Endorsements and Testimonials: Be careful not to use reviews, testimonials, or endorsements in a misleading or dishonest way in your content. Verify that testimonials adhere to advertising guidelines and standards and are sincere, truthful, and representative of real user experiences.

Accessibility: Comply with online accessibility standards and guidelines, such as the online Content Accessibility Guidelines (WCAG), to make your blog accessible to people with impairments. Make sure that people with motor, cognitive, visual, or auditory impairments can access your blog's functionality, design, and content.

Maintain a high standard of ethical behavior and professionalism while interacting with your readers, other bloggers, brands, and colleagues in the field. In all of your blogging endeavors, conduct yourself with honesty, decency, and openness. Refrain from using dishonest, immoral, or manipulative tactics.

Building trust with your audience, protecting your reputation, and developing a successful and long-lasting blogging career may all be achieved by placing a high priority on ethical behavior, legal compliance, and responsible blogging practices. Keep yourself up to date on all applicable laws, rules, and industry standards. If you have any questions regarding compliance matters or any legal ramifications, get legal counsel.

Future Blogging Trends

Future blogging trends will depend on a number of factors, including changing user behavior, developing industry dynamics, and emerging technologies. Although it's difficult to predict every move, the following are some possible directions that blogging may take in the future:

Video blogging, also known as vlogging, is expected to grow in popularity within the blogging community due to the growing appeal of video content on social media platforms and streaming services. In order to interact with their audience through visual storytelling, bloggers can include videos in their posts or switch to vlogging channels.

Bloggers may consider experimenting with interactive and immersive content forms, such virtual reality (VR), augmented reality (AR), or interactive storytelling experiences, as technology develops. By adding immersive aspects, blog experiences can become more effective and memorable for users.

Microblogging and Short-form Content: Due to their capacity to provide easily absorbed content in bite-sized chunks, short-form content platforms such as Instagram, TikTok, and Twitter have become increasingly popular. Microblogging is a format that bloggers can use to convey brief updates, thoughts, or material snippets that appeal to the fast-paced digital audience of today.

Niche and Specialized Content: In an effort to stand out from the competition and appeal to particular audience groups, bloggers may choose to concentrate on niche subjects or specialized content categories as the blogging market grows more crowded. Within well-known niches, micro-niches may form that enable bloggers to focus on incredibly narrow passions and interests.

Voice Search Optimization: Blogging communities may give priority to voice search optimization in order to increase the discoverability of their material through voice inquiries, given the increasing popularity of speech-activated gadgets and virtual assistants such as Google Assistant and Amazon Alexa. Search visibility can be increased and voice search traffic can be drawn by optimizing for natural language and conversational questions.

Customization and Personalization: Using data analytics, AI, and machine learning algorithms, bloggers may tailor product offers, user experiences, and content recommendations to each individual reader depending on their tastes, habits, and demographics. User engagement and loyalty can be increased by customizing material to their interests.

E-commerce Integration: Through product sales, affiliate marketing, or sponsored partnerships, bloggers can directly monetise their content by looking at e-commerce integration opportunities. Blog entries that include shopping features, product suggestions, and affiliate links can increase income streams and improve user experience when it comes to making purchases.

Collaborative Content & Community Building: Bloggers can host collaborative events, co-create content, or take part in cross-promotional activities in partnership with businesses, influencers, or other content creators. Collaborating, being creative, and engaging an audience can all be encouraged by creating communities based on common interests and beliefs.

Ethical and Sustainable Blogging Practices: As social and environmental issues get more attention, bloggers may place a higher priority on ethical and sustainable blogging techniques include openly disclosing sponsored content, consuming and producing material responsibly, and supporting social causes. Socially conscious viewers may connect with material and projects that emphasize sustainability.

The increasing prevalence of mobile devices may prompt bloggers to give priority to mobile optimization and accessibility in order to guarantee that their material is readable and navigable on a wide range of screens and devices. The mobile surfing experience can be enhanced by using responsive web design strategies and mobile-first design concepts.

Bloggers may stay ahead of the curve and succeed in the dynamic and ever-changing blogging landscape by keeping up with developing trends, experimenting with new technology, and adjusting to altering audience preferences.

Summary

In summary, discovering the keys to profitable blogging necessitates a multidimensional approach that includes planning, imagination, and commitment. Bloggers must accept new trends, overcome obstacles, and maintain moral principles in order to create successful, long-lasting blogs that connect with their readers. Bloggers may discover the keys to success and realize their blogging objectives by concentrating on important components including high-quality material, engaged audiences, effective monetization techniques, and legal compliance.

Effective blogging is more than just producing material; it also entails developing connections, adding value, and having a significant influence in your industry. It's about providing insightful content on a regular basis, encouraging community involvement, and making adjustments to meet the changing demands and tastes of your audience. It's about remaining real, staying loyal to your brand, and always pushing the boundaries of innovation and progress.

We predict that new technology, trends, and opportunities will emerge in the future, reshaping the blogging landscape and presenting bloggers with both chances and difficulties. In the ever-changing realm of blogging, bloggers can thrive by remaining proactive, flexible, and open-minded.

Ultimately, passion, perseverance, and purpose are the keys to a great blog. It's about speaking up, expressing your distinct viewpoint, and adding something worthwhile to the online community. Regardless of your level of experience, success as a blogger is determined by the connections and effect you create along the journey rather than by awards or stats. Thus, continue to write, continue to learn, and continue to share the secrets of profitable blogging. The benefits of the voyage are limitless, despite its challenges.

THE END

www.ingramcontent.com/pod-product-compliance
Lightning Source LLC
Chambersburg PA
CBHW070201230526
45471CB00002B/765